The Old Yellow House

By Joyce Wright

The Old Yellow House

Copyright © 2018 by Joyce Wright

ISBN-13: 978-1-944583-25-5

Contact:

Email: theoldyellowhouse@outlook.com

Published by Laurel Rose Publishing

www.laurelrosepublishing.com

laurelrosepublishing@gmail.com

Joyce Wright

Names have been changed to protect the identities of those who wish to remain anonymous.

Table of Contents

PREFACE.. 5

CHAPTER 1 13

CHAPTER 2 17

CHAPTER 3.. 25

CHAPTER 4.. 37

CHAPTER 5.. 43

CHAPTER 6.. 47

CHAPTER 7.. 51

CHAPTER 8.. 64

CHAPTER 9.. 77

CHAPTER 10... 85

CHAPTER 11... 91

PART 2 THIS WORLD WE LIVE IN 102

CHAPTER 12.. 103

CHAPTER 13.. 121

PREFACE

Before I begin telling the story of the "Old Yellow House", let me give a little background which could possibly concern why the house was possessed or if you prefer the saying, haunted. It could be something that my family brought into the space, or maybe it could already have been there and was triggered by our presence. This I will get into on the second section of this publication. But until that time, let me tell a brief history as I know it to be first.

First I need to explain why I call the house yellow. It really is simple; that is the color I chose when we painted it. Seems that the house was always white. And I say 'seems' because what was left of the dilapidated house was bare wood. It was amazing that it wasn't rotten, being we live in termite territory, with no protective cover on it. But it was what it was, just an old, fancy looking, farm house, nothing more. I bet in its hay days, it was a sight to see.

The scroll work on the front porch and eves of the gable roof, the nine foot windows, the eleven foot ceiling, the solid wood construction, the pine floors, the plastered wall and ceilings, the three porches, cedar shake roof (which had been replaced somewhere in the past) and the thick, solid wood doors made this place unique.

The front door was a piece of art. Half of the door was a window. I didn't like the idea of anyone just coming up and looking into our house, so I designed a stained glass window and commissioned it to be constructed. It really set off the front of the house with the Iris depiction in greens and lavender. I even had a peep hole done in one of the buds on the stems. To this day, I have no idea what happened to that glass. Sad.

My brief research of the history of this house, came mainly from several neighbors who were born and raised in Tyro. Just about everyone here in close proximity had lived here since birth. So the info I received came from childhood memories through adulthood. To begin with, I had no idea that just before we moved here, the street had been paved (from the gravel road it had always been). That seems odd that it took that long to accomplish since this road was the 'main street'. Most of the businesses were located on this thoroughfare.

Also, which might shock some people, is that we were one of the first families to get a private line for our phone service. Up until this time in the early 1980's, everyone in this area had to rely on what they called party lines. For those of you who are unfamiliar with this term, it means you are connected with several other families to form your service. So when you ordered a phone into your home, (and yes, it was a privilege back in the 'dark ages'), most had to share one line. You could pick up your receiver to make a call and there might already be someone on the phone. Even when the phone rang at your home, each house had a specific cadence to let you know if it was your residence that someone was calling.

For example: one ring and a pause would be the 'Smith's" number. Two rings and a pause would be the 'Jones' number. Two fast rings and a long ring would be your ring number. That way every time the phone rang, you'd know when to answer.

BUT, if you happened to be a busybody or one of your neighbors was a gossiper, he or she could pick up and listen to your conversation. Most people, though back then, didn't have time to eavesdrop on their neighbors. There was just too many chores to do. So we were "privileged" at that time in the early 80's, to actually have a private phone and an asphalt road in front of our new home.

From what I could glean from our neighbors, this house went through several different families. The first residence they could remember was a doctor and his family. It seems strange that at one time, Tyro was a thriving little town with many business'. I don't know what the reason was for the house to change occupants, but it ended up being sold, and the Brantley family was the family who next owned the property.

If you lived here in the northwest corner of Mississippi, you might be familiar with Brantley Funeral Home in Hernando. Yes, this was the family who lived in the old yellow house for years. Not , of course, the ones alive at this writing, but the matriarchs of the business. From what I could gather from my neighbors who know the family, they were well respected.

Back at that time of history, some people had tenant houses on their property. This is where the help lived rent free. Their jobs were to either help farm, keep the property up, sometimes cook, "AND" the Brantley's actually had a butler! Now don't get too excited about the helps plight. They did get wages, somewhat. This also joined in with what families called 'sharecropper' experience. Just know one thing: this is not my call. I never fit into such a category of having experienced this type of situation.

Back to their butler. The tenant house, plus another one still stood on our place when we acquired it. I was told the family that helped with the grounds had lived in the two room cabin that stood back behind our barn. Whereas, the butlers residence was east of the barn next to a pond. Both were somewhat visible from the back of the house. The butler's residence actually consisted of three rooms. That was unique for the size and seemed privileged from what I was told.

The culture I encountered once we finally got the house livable to move into, was a real surprise to me. I had lived both in the country and in the city. When living in the country, I'd classify how I was raised as dirt poor. We had electricity for lights and the one refrigerator. We had no running water, not inside toilet, wood heat, and my mom and granddad cooked on a wood stove. So I never saw the likes of what I was told in the Tyro community. I even found out that most of the women did not do laundry. There was a family down the road that set up times for whatever families wanted to use them, to wash, dry and iron their clothes. Later on after we were there, the person passed and the women in the community broke down and bought washers and dryers and began doing their own laundry. I don't know about you, but that seemed out of my league since I always took care of my own stuff.

Another anomaly I discovered upon moving to Tyro was that the men took care of everything outside, including the garden. Where I was from, my mom, my aunts, cousins, etc, all women, did the gardening and canning. So when I moved there and began my gardening and yard work, I was looked upon like I was from outer space or had two heads. Most of the neighbors didn't understand that I loved to work in the soil myself. Nothing feels better to me than digging and getting my hands dirty. It is a pleasure to put seeds in the ground, watch your plants grow, harvest the fruit, then can or freeze the harvest. To me that is an accomplishment, plus it does help to feed your family.

One last thing I learned along the way. One day my husband and I happened to go by to ask my neighbor, Mrs. Johnson, something. She had stepped outside to look at her flowers in the front flower bed. We had not called to let her know that we were coming since we were not going to stay but just long enough to ask the question.

Upon seeing us pull up in the driveway, she made a beeline into her house and not too long after entering, she emerged and greeted us. What she immediately told us was that she was barefooted and ran in to put on her shoes. "OK, I thought. What was the big deal of putting on you shoes?"

Have you ever heard the old saying, "barefoot and pregnant"? I never knew what that phrase actually meant until that moment. She explained (not that she was pregnant with her age. After all, she was a grandmother), men could not see women barefoot and she had walked outside barefoot to look at her flowers. Back in the olden days, that phrase had come into being while women were to be hidden if they were with child. I know, that seems funny nowadays, but that was the way it was. So if you took away your woman's shoes, or if she were pregnant, she was stuck indoors, not being able to been seen in a public setting. Only the 'loose' women did such a thing by showing off their feet. Funny, huh? I love to go barefooted and I hope no man gets a wrong idea, or has a foot fetish. Thank goodness for at least that change in our society that women can go barefooted and it is not a sin.

Okay, I've diverted enough so back to the Brantley's. All I remember that the neighbors telling me is that when Mr. Brantley passed, they had his funeral in the living room. They stood his casket right in front of the three windows that form a curve out from the house. Whether the preaching service was held there or in a church, I haven't a clue.

So as far as I know, there is the first dead body on the premises. Where he passed, that I cannot tell you.

The second death I know for sure happened on the property. That would be the Meek family, who we bought the property from. Mr. Meek was a widower. He and his wife never had children, so the estate went to his brothers and sisters. I believe there were a total of 6, but don't quote me on that. So when the house sold to us, they split the proceeds between them. Two of his sisters were our neighbors. In fact, one of their properties ran a long side our place. I will tell more within the chapters later on the book. But for now, let's set the stage for maybe why, how, when, and what has happened throughout my life and with others I have shared a common bond with.

CHAPTER 1

I have always been fascinated with the unknown as far back as I can remember. Only trouble was, everyone I was associated with put down any superstitious thinking, ghosts, supernatural, physic thinking, etc. that I had. No on actual called it witchcraft or demons, or even miracles. They just pashawed it and didn't want to hear about it. Some actually made fun of me, belittling me to the point that I just shut up and never tried to discuss my curiosity.

With that said, I was a late bloomer to all my experiences. And still then, I didn't have the guts to voice my opinion or what I actually believed and saw.

My imagination would run wild when I was beginning school. The schools up north were run far different than the one in the south. We had field trips to wild west forts with actual stage coach rides, movies, orchestra concerts and even had swimming lessons given to us.

The movies were really my first look into the 'supernatural'. Being a very impressionable child, I believed what I saw. Cinderella and fairy godmothers, with singing birds and pumpkin carriages was the real deal.   Poof, and there it would appear.

Snow White, asleep for who knows how long, was as real as real could be for me. The evil stepmother in both films was doing an act I didn't like. Putting spells on innocent young girls was uncalled for. After all, what had they ever done to them except exist? How could they be so cruel? Peter Pan was it for me. You could fly. Really fly. And when Keds sneakers had commercials about flying with them on, and to top it, my mom making me a Peter Pan costume----I mean----how could I go wrong?

But try and try again, jumping off the front stoop of our duplex; jumping off chairs in the house; even thinking if people didn't see me in the bathroom jumping off the toilet, it just had to work. Each time I tried, believing even harder each time that it would work, what a great disappointment. Why was I lied to?

So, I gave up all ideas at this point.....for now.

As I entered the later year in elementary school, we moved back to the south. The area we lived in had a movie theater close by. So on Saturday afternoons, my daddy would drive me to the matinee to see movies. That's the time all the movies about the beach with Annette Funicello and Frankie Avalon were on. But laced within these teenage beach parties would be Edgar Allan Poe, Vincent Price, Bela Lugosi and Boris Karloff movies.

The scare tactics were real for me and it would take me several nights to get over the fright of the dark. I never told my parents, for if I did, I'd never be taken to another picture show as I was under their roof. There was even a time that I decided to be an archaeologist. I still to this day think that it is a fascinating form of profession. What stopped me from pursuing that profession was one movie---The Mummy. I know you are laughing at me right now for admitting this, but all you had to convince me was a 'curse' placed on anyone who opened a tomb. That did it for me. No way was I going to dig up any remains and have such a thing spoken over me and my family.

This is how vulnerable, impressionable, and sensitive I was to scripts. No one was going to convince me it was not real. And I didn't want any problems. Another movie that held magical implications for me was a Santa Claus movie. Don't laugh. I really believed in this guy. After all, my parents wouldn't just tell me a bald face lie would they? Come on, there was even a tooth fairy and an Easter Bunny. This magic reel was real! Money and presents! What else could a child want?

In the movies, this Santa could just POOF! And He'd be in and out of houses at the blink of an eye. So here I go again believing what adults were portraying as real. Little did I realize, years later, my bubble in the supernatural realm would again be burst. When my parents sat me down and told me there was no such thing as Santa, the Easter Bunny, or the tooth fairy, I not only was devastated, but wanted to die. And that they were the gift givers! How cruel can you get? It took me a long period of time to get over this set back. I was numb and my innocence was lost. I was now old enough to know the truth is what they told me. Truth? What is truth when adults lie to you? Are you feeling it? And what is sooooo sad, my husband and I carried on the same "tradition" and taught those lies to our children! Are we all sick, morbid, or what? Does everyone get a kick out of this? What else have we been told lies about? Think about that.

CHAPTER 2

I love to work with my hands. Regardless of what it is, I feel satisfaction during any project and especially upon completion. But then, there is a dilemma; what's my next project? So when it came to schooling, I fit right in to the subjects offered of Home Economics, Art and yes...shop.

Home Economics awarded me with the satisfaction of cooking, cleaning, and sewing. And also, I like to clean and reorganize (missed my calling). My mom and my father's father were both Tailors. So, I guess it is in the blood. I've been sewing since I was twelve years old and for short periods in my life, actually sewed for the public. I even designed clothes and entered contest back in high school. Along with doing that, I fit right into art class, which was actually my major.

My intent towards my looking into colleges was to be an Interior Decorator. That's another story in itself that I will not go into, but it never panned out. I only ended up decorating for friends and family. I never did it professionally or ever had a 'degree' to show. But along the path I've taken, there have been experiences. I ended up marrying into a family of carpenters. And this was not only someone who built subdivisions, but a family who was before their time. I'm saying here the original "This Old House", Bob Villa type. They would get a down and out house either by purchasing or trading and remodel the entire property and then sell it with a profit. So when I married into the family that is exactly the course we took. The longest we ever lived in a house was for four years.

Now, let's get back to the High School years. The technique I was being taught in Art class and Drafting, (had to have this course in architecture to design), perked my curiosity in restoration and designing.

Stay with me now. I have to set the stage to what happened to me.

I know little or almost close to nothing about my father's side of the family. I don't know why I was in my parent's bedroom closet, but I discovered two large portraits I had never seen before. With not dragging them out of the closet, I went and asked my mother what and who they were. One was a photo of my grandfather, his son (my father), and his daughter. It was maybe 1920ish, and everyone actually had on boots that buttoned up. I'd say my father, sitting on his father's lap, was about two or three years old.

The other was a portrait of a woman in her 20's, a very distinguished, beautiful person. She was posing what looked like an elaborate chair or chaise of wood and leather. The side of the back was ornately carved and rounded at the top. She was sitting on the side, since it had no arms, with one arm in her lap and the other arm propped up on the back of the chair. Her elbow was bent and her hand was resting on the back of her head. This may sound as if it was somewhat sexy in nature, but it is not. It portrayed simply a resting position since she was casual, with the look on her face as if she were reminiscing. The photo was large, 16"x20", with the frame making it even bigger since it was matted. I'm not sure what they call the finish, but it is all browns, no color.

Her dress was that of the early 1900's. Her skirt was to the floor. Her blouse was full and long, bellowing through the front. There was either tatting or crochet collar that covered from her neck, halfway down the front of her blouse. She wore white gloves that extended half way up her forearm and edged with the same tattering or crochet edging that gave them a four inch ruffling effect. The hair was long and styled out away from her face and brought back into a bun at the back of her head. I believe they called this a chignon hairstyle.

I asked my mother, "Who in the world is this lady?" That is when I found out that that lady was my father's mother, my grandmother. What a shock, since I grew up never ever knowing either of my grandmothers. Both had passed before I was born. But now I found out that even my father didn't have the privilege of knowing his mother but for a short time. She had passed when he was very young, probably not too long after that portrait had been made.

The frame was ornate and coming to pieces. I doubt if it was real gold leaf, but the surfaces of the carvings on the frame were gold color. Some of the pieces had dislodged and were barely hanging onto the frame. With the fascination of my discovery, the mystery of the woman, the elaborate dress and frame, I needed that portrait hanging in my room. It would go with my decor that I was shooting for in the decorating of my space, which just happened to be my bedroom there at home.

In art class I had learned about some techniques in restoration. So I was on the move now to attempt to restore this frame, clean the glass that covered the portrait, and hang this gem of a find over my daybed.

With my parent's permission, the task was completed and over the daybed the picture went. My first night after the picture was hung, I slept pretty restless. The same happened again the second night. I just chalked it up to anxiety, or maybe something I had ate before retiring.

But the real clincher happened on the third night. I found myself in the throes of a nightmare. Tossing and turning, I finally awoken. I was lying on my back, so when I opened my eyes, I would be looking up at the ceiling. Let me insert here that my bedroom was in the corner of the house. Right outside my front window was a street light. So, my room was not pitch black. With that said, what I was about to experience scared the living daylights out of me.

Coming out of that photo of my grandmother, was what seem to be smoke. It could be also said that it looked something like a cloud. The hole was not even the size of a dime. But as it poured out, it expanded as if it were attempting to fill my bedroom.

Ok, now is the time to freak out. I didn't do anything to cause alarm in my house. Remember, I was made fun of when it came to stuff like this. I was the one with the vivid imagination. So what I did was hide; hide under the covers and hope that it would just go away. I know this sounds stupid, but it is what it is. That was my protection. I'm really putting myself out here for ridicule, but this is the truth.

When finally everyone was awake in the house, (I got absolutely no sleep after the episode), I got the picture off the wall. I then snuck it back into my parent's closet, shutting the door to any abnormal anomalies that might try to frighten me while sleeping in my bed. I thought, 'Case closed on that experience."

I felt that episode would be dead and buried. But, days later, my mother questioned me on how the portrait had ended back into her closet. Having to quickly come up with an excuse without explaining the real reason, I told her that I had decided that it did not go with the decor I was shooting for. She didn't question me any further, believing my lame excuse. What a relief.

I have to this date, never figured out what happened or why. I can expound that maybe my grandmother was reaching out from the grave trying to contact me? Was there something attached to that portrait? Was there something I did personally that drew this 'entity' into my room? Did I bring anything home that an entity had attached itself to and was exposing itself to me? Your guess is as good as mine.

After that, my sleep went back to normal and I had no further episodes.

The Old Yellow House

CHAPTER 3

You're about to think I'm crazy now. Maybe I am, but my next experience with the supernatural began with the parlor game called a Ouija Board. Still fascinated with the here and after aspect of life, I was still looking for answers from the unseen world. I know there has to be another reality or dimension. After all, it states in the Bible how prophets and ordinary people saw angels and apparitions and even experienced miracles in their day and time. So, why would it be any different now? What has changed? In my view, absolutely nothing. Jesus even stated that greater things you will do and see. Do I take Him at His Word? Some people do while others say it's all over. I guess then that we are all on our own? Good luck, hope you make it out safely?

Well, I don't see how we can be left to fend for ourselves. For me, I want answers and I'm willing to search and seek wherever and whatever it may take to find it, within reason.

When I was around fifteen years old, I'd heard about the Ouija Board. If it was worked properly, it would answer any question posed towards it. Just maybe this was where I could finally get some of my questions answered. So, I asked my parents to buy me one and much to their chagrin, they bought one for me. They hadn't a clue what a Ouija Board was. They thought it was just a board game just like all the other games my brother and I had in the house. Neither myself nor my parents knew about any repercussions that could arise from playing with it. And facts be known, neither did any of my friends. We all felt it was a spoof, just fun and games.

I really do not remember how I even heard about a Ouija Board. No one I knew had one, so I'd be the first one to delve into this experience. When I got it, it seemed rather odd. There was a solid board colored a light beige with black letters and symbols printed on it. The alphabet went across the center which was made up on several lines. The sun was in the upper left corner and moon was in the upper right corner. The word 'yes' was next to the sun and word 'no' was up next to the moon. Below the alphabet were numbers one through zero. Goodbye was written across the middle of the bottom under the numbers.

There was an odd shaped device called a planchette that sat on three short legs that was to be the object of communication. On it was a clear, round window that if looked through, one would be able to see what the device was answering to the question posed. So my friends and I were novices jumping into the unknown like babes fed to the wolves.

So now, let me set the stage of events.

My best friend, Melanie, moved to another town right after school let out for the summer break. I was moping around the remainder of the summer vacation with no one to hang around with. When school began, at least I had my time occupied now. But it was not by what I called an ideal situation. I really didn't care much for school. I love to learn and read, but hated the set-up of the politics and institution that goes with the territory. Since I was in junior high, we changed classes throughout the day after spending fifteen minutes in homeroom. There in my homeroom was a new student named Sharon. You'd have to realize that very few newcomers came to our school. So, they more or less stuck out like a sore thumb---very well noticed. At first, the new student would be extremely popular until they fit into a certain 'clique'. And once they are in that 'clique', the new wore off and it would be school as usual.

Sharon was a natural blonde, shoulder length hair, a few bangs, average size, and wore these cat eye glasses. No one would ever guess that if she took her glasses off, she was beautiful. But for now, all you saw were these awful glasses with a girl hiding behind them.

As weeks passed, we began to talk and found out that she lived only two blocks from my house. Well we struck up a friendship immediately after that discovery and we were inseparable from that moment onward. When I would be over at her house, her older sister, Charlotte, had her best friend over whose name was Virginia.

So now, in the scenario, steps in my Ouija Board. We all four attempted to try to make the thing work as the instructions said it would. But, no cigar. None of us singularly or corporately could get the planchette to work. So, back in my closet it went.

If Sharon and Charlotte's mom ever found out what we were up to with that board, it would have been hell to pay. You, see, their mom was a very religious woman. She once told Virginia and me the story of her experience.

She had gone into the hospital for an operation. During it, while on the table, she died. In however long her heart was not beating and the surgeon was attempting to revive her, she says she went to heaven and spoke to Jesus. She begged Him to allow her to return back to earth to raise her three children. (there was also a younger brother). Of course, you'll know the answer, since she was sitting there telling us this story. With that, you can just imagine how she'd feel if she found out we were playing with a spirit board. After all, that was the work of the devil. And who really knows, maybe it is?

Well, we were all best friends for around a year and a half when Sharon's parents decided to move back to Indiana. Virginia and my hearts were broken. We were losing our best friends.

I had to tell you all this, so you can see how Virginia and I became best friends. She was just one year older than me. I seemed to always have friends older than me. She also lived a little further from me. So, when we'd go over to one another's home, we'd call each other to say we were leaving, start walking, and meet each other halfway. Then we'd proceed to whoever's house we were hanging out at. You can probably tell that this took place a long time ago when people walked with no fear of harm.

Virginia lived in what one would call a low income neighborhood. Not that we lived in a high class one, but ours was what I'd call a lower middle class. My father was a carrier for the Postal Service. Neither one of our mothers worked outside the home. I'm not sure what Virginia's father did for a living, but the one thing I do know is he was an alcoholic and her mom was of a Pentecostal religious belief. Complete opposites were they. She was always praying to get him sober and saved. And her father was rebelling as much as possible. So there stuck in the middle was Virginia, an older brother , and a younger sister.

My parents did not approve of my newly found friend. They had probably heard that the police visited Virginia's house frequently. When her dad drank, he'd use her mom as a punching bag. I never saw or experienced this, but you can understand why my folks disapproved. As a means of escape, we'd walk and sit around listening to music.

One Sunday after being board out of our minds, we decided to break out the Ouija and give it a try. The planets and the stars must have been in the right alignment, because the board was actually working! But, that was a big BUT, for little did we know how we were playing with fire and opening up doors which needed to remain shut.

We didn't burn candles or anything like that trying to get into the mood, scenario. We did have the curtains drawn and a lamp on, even though it was a bright, sunny day. Her room was on the north side of the house and there were large trees in their backyard. It was in the middle of summer, so her room seemed to always remain with a dim amount of natural light. So in order to see properly, we'd have to have some form of lighting. After all, how would we be able to read the board.

So, here we are, babes in the woods, not understanding the dangers we were putting ourselves into. After all, they sell these games in any store that sells toys. So what could go wrong or what danger could one step into? Right?

Well, we read the instructions, with skepticism. Then laughed and joked about what would or would not happen.

We began by introducing ourselves to the spirit world. An announcement, that we were here, willing and able to receive answers from the great beyond. Boy, what a big mistake. (in hindsight) Then as the instructions directed, we placed our fingertips on the planchette and waited. And we waited and we waited. Curiosity of the unknown in our immature minds and ways was getting the best of us.

So, what seemed like an eternity, nothing was happening. We took our fingertips off the planchette, sat back in our chairs and decided to regroup. Was this game just a hoax or were we doing something wrong? Maybe we didn't have enough faith in the board or the spirit world realm. The answers were just not coming.

We had nothing else to do with our time, so we decided to approach the board from a different angle. This time, we'll antagonize the spirit realm into answering us. Thus, we sat forward and placed our fingertips once more upon the planchette. This time we began to mock any entity that might be hovering around the vicinity. We were trying to get anything or anyone just to get this board to work. Just like any normal, red blooded teenager, we wanted proof of their existence.

Slowly, we felt the movement. Accusing each other of pushing the planchette on the board, we finally came to the conclusion that it really was working this time. The questions now began to pour out of our mouths and as fast as we could ask them, the answers would be immediately appear. At first they were simple yes or no answers to our questions. But as time progressed, the answers we asked became more complicated in that the alphabet on the board was used to spell them out.

Intrigued and yet scared out of our wits, we trudged on with as many serious and silly questions we could think up. With no idea how long this had gone on, things now were becoming quite serious in nature.

We were becoming exhausted with every step we took towards the supernatural. It seemed that it was getting harder to concentrate and to even breath. How much time elapsed, we're not sure. But, it did seem that it was towards twilight within that bedroom.

At that moment, the whole atmosphere changed. A fog seemed to be enveloping us. This seemed to be the reason it was getting harder and harder to breath. The planchette was shaking and acting as if it had a mind of its own. I'm not sure who did it first, but we both eventually took our hands off of it AND the object continued to spell out words on its own. It was actually moving on that board with an invisibility we could not detect. We could only feel its presence. The filth that was being spewed out in the spelling on the board was now outrageous.

Virginia and I looked up, with fright, at each other. We then bolted from that room and didn't stop until we reached the middle of the road she lived on. Her street was a quiet, back road area with little traffic. We stopped, turned around to view her house, not knowing what we were going to see.

To our amazement, all seemed peaceful. The sun was shining, a light breeze was blowing through the trees, and the birds were chirping. All seemed at peace. Not even her parents or sister came out of that house at breakneck speed.

Taking in deep breaths, we wandered over to the curb and sat down. Neither one of us spoke a word. We just sat contemplating on what we had experienced and the next big question ----- what to do now? You know, I look back and feel so sorry for both of us. One: Virginia's room was where all this took place. How was she ever going to go back in there, much less sleep in it. Two: I had the board game. I now had to retrieve it, take it home, and deal with its presence.

It was getting late and now was time for me to head back home. We had to both gather up enough courage to go back into her bedroom, and get that 'game'. So off we went. On arrival into the room, at first we just peered into it, like one would do to see if the coast were clear. To our amazement, the room looked normal. No smoke or fog seemed to be present in the atmosphere.

The light was as bright as it normally was. The board sat on the table just as still as could be.

I grabbed the box, placed the board and planchette in, shut the lid, placed it under my arm, and out the door of her bedroom and house we walked. Not a word was said between us. We always walked to meet or leave each other halfway. So when we got to our destination, Virginia turned and walked back home as I continued to my house.

Once arriving home, I went straight to my room, opened my closet door, and put the Ouija Board as far back into my closet as I possibly could. I figured, 'out of sight, out of mind'. Until I had some answers to what had just happened that afternoon, that thing would remain in the back of my closet.

But who could I ask? I know, maybe I could put feelers out at school and see what would happen. We'd see then, when school began if we could come up with a solution.

The Old Yellow House

CHAPTER 4

My life from that point would be described as a typical, growing up, in the south, USA teenager and young adult years. This took place in the 60's and 70's. I got married at what some may call a young age, and started a family. Just to keep on track with the subject of this book, I never dabbled with my Ouija Board since that incident. But I still was being drawn, not that often I might add, to the supernatural. I'd pick up an occasional book to glance at, really not knowing why. I also felt drawn to certain people who seemed to be able to look into the unseen realm. But, that's the extent of about fifteen years of my young adult life. My time was occupied with family.

In the early 1980's, circumstances presented themselves to us once we had been living in Mississippi for around five years. We had a chance to buy an old homestead, cheap I might add, in the southeast corner of the county below from where we were living at the time. The man who had passed, was a widow and never sired any children. So, the property went to his brothers and sisters. They in turn, opted to sell said property and then divide the proceeds amongst themselves.

With that in mind, we were negotiating back and forth about the purchase price. I can't remember how many weeks it took us, but finally, a price was decided upon, and the ball now, was literally in our court to accept or deny it.

This was a huge decision. We'd be a little further from any family members. We knew absolutely no one there at all. It was a move from the schools the kids attended. But, with all that said, the house was close to 100 years old and had been totally, and I do mean TOTALLY, neglected. It was not livable. It would take us months, working every day, just to get it to the point that we could "camp out" in it and try to finish the work. But, I do love challenges and could see the potential of this place. Also, in that time of my life, I was hooked on homesteading.

We had chickens, quail, rabbits, a pony, and milk goats. All this would need to be transported to our new property upon completion. Plus, we'd be working on two places now. The one we were living in would have to be spruced up to sell, not to mention taking care of the livestock. Then we'd spend as much as we could, time wise, to fix this old house.

By now, you probable guess, that we bought the place. The final papers were signed in

March and by the time school began in August, we were in it. I'm not going to say that it was completed, because it was far from it. But at least we could camp out in it. And boy, what a move it was with all the animals.

You know what though? I wouldn't trade it for the world. It was a real experience and we were happy as a lark.

Until........

We'd been in the house now around a year. This community was the best and I say that sincerely. The people living here were actually born and raised here. It was a step back in time. Everyone knew everyone; everyone helped out everyone who needed it. Even the two churches worked together. There was a Baptist and a Methodist church. The Baptist met most Sundays. But the Methodist didn't have a congregation large enough to support a full time pastor. So they had it was on a circuit. Mt. Vernon Methodist Church met most Sundays. Freedonia Methodist Church met the first Sunday of every month. And Tyro Methodist Church met the third Sunday, which meant the other two churches were closed. What was so unique at the time, was when Tyro Methodist Church met, The Baptist Church closed it doors and most of the congregation were at the

Methodist church, (I found out that those who attended were actually Methodist and just didn't want to drive those extra miles to attend the others. So they attended the Baptist Church instead.)

I hope I didn't confuse you in all this explaining. I'm just trying to let you know how close knit a community Tyro was.

This place use to be a thriving town. I learned it had stores, gas stations, a creamery, doctors, etc. What killed the growth was the Railroad. It ended up going through Senatobia, which caused all of the economy to head into that direction. This county was actually part of Desoto County until it was voted on to separate, due to the flooding of the Coldwater River.

Each spring, when the rains would come, people couldn't make it to the county seat of Hernando to pay their property taxes. So they voted to separate, and thus became the county of Tate. And you can guess where the county line separated, right along the Coldwater River.

I've digressed some. But I had to in order to set the stage for what was about to be exposed.

I'm not sure what spawned the events. Maybe they were already happening, but on a less noticeable scale. I cannot really say for sure. I'm also not sure exactly which event happened first. So, I'll just start with the cold spots.

The Old Yellow House

CHAPTER 5

This house I call the old yellow house, only because that is the color we chose to paint it. It was rather fancy on the exterior; known as a Victorian style farmhouse. But inside was another story. It was built back in the days, when the kitchens were at the rear of the dwelling due to the heat of the summer. They cooked on wood cook stoves. The kitchen had five doors. Four lead to the outer porches on three sides and one lead towards the front of the house into what served as a dining room. This was a typical floorplan for that era.

Since it was so chopped up, there left little, to no, wall space. My hot water tank was in the corner closest to a hall that had originally been a porch. It had been enclosed to form a room six feet wide, by 30 feet long. By the time we had acquired the house, two doors leading out to the back porch had been closed over to allow for cabinets and a sink.

Next to the heater was my stove to cook on. No other wall space would allow for our refrigerator. So, we did the next best thing and placed it in the hall right next to the door leading into the kitchen. To draw you a better picture, so there is no doubt in your mind's, I was almost in arms-length from the stove to the refrigerator. No more than two or three steps between me and it. Get the picture? Oh, by the way, I had a wood cook stove in the center of the kitchen to cook on, which I used during the winter months (makes the best biscuits).

The house was arranged for the turn of the century era living, and it was next to impossible to cool, much less heat this house without a central unit. We decided not to put that much money into this house feeling it was not worth it. Plus, in the summer, with the eleven foot tall ceiling and ceiling fans in every room, this house wasn't bad; unless, you were canning vegetables or making jelly.

On this particular day, that is exactly what I was doing; canning. Being in the summer time, school was out. Along with our two children, there were nine other kids in the neighborhood. This day two of the kids were over and all four were in and out of the house all day long.

When it would get too hot, we did have a window air conditioner unit at the front part of the house. But with the floor plan, we had to shut off the front rooms for it to work properly. That left the kitchen, back hall, and dining room on its own with no relief other than a box fan.

So, I'm standing in front of the stove canning. Sweat is pouring off of me. I turn to walk across the floor to go over to the sink. It's about three steps away. When I return to the stove, I step into a spot of extremely, cold air. I'm baffled. Where did this cold air come from? It feels like the freezer when you stand at it with the door open. It is so cold, I actually had goosebumps. For some reason I think one of the kids left the refrigerator door open and that's what I'm experiencing. I look at this explanation and think how stupid can I be, but look I must to see if it is the case. After all, it's an arms-length away.

I look. No, it is closed tight. So, in all my confusion, I stand back in front of the stove and there it still is. Now I find myself stepping in and stepping out to this cold spot. I'm really now looking for answers. Could the cold have come back from the front of the house when possibly the kids left the door open between the two sections of the house? So I go to investigate.

No, the doors are all closed and the kids are out in the yard playing. I call for Don, my husband, explaining this phenomenon.

He steps into the spot and is just as puzzled as I am. So, he also goes to investigate the refrigerator, freezers, and front part of the house.

Upon his return back into the kitchen, he can still experience this cold spot right in front of the stove.

The kids now come in and are wondering what we are doing. We explain to them and then they begin stepping into the cold spot and out of it. They of course thought it was cool, but still strange. Later on when other things began happening in our home, the neighborhood kids just took it in stride. After all, how cool is it to know someone in your neighborhood that lives in a haunted house.

We have no idea how long this lasted. But just as quick as it manifested, it left. To this day, we have no explanation of what this 'cold spot' phenomenon was or is. But this was only the beginning of many strange things that happened at The Old Yellow House.

CHAPTER 6

Other experiences began to emerge not only with me, but my children and some of their friends.

I remember several times either being in the yard, or driving up the driveway and seeing an elderly man digging in the flowerbed at the front of the house. Puzzled, I glanced away and when I looked back, he was gone. None of the dirt had been disturbed where I had seen him. Along with this sighting, one of my daughter Linell's friends, Kaye, was over one day. I'm here going to note that these events took place in broad daylight. I was in the kitchen when Kaye came into the room wanting to know if Linell's grandfather was spending the night. Okay, another puzzling sighting since neither one of our fathers were at the house.

I asked her why she was asking that? She commenced to tell me about the elderly man sitting in the living room, in my husband's recliner, reading a newspaper. Well, I immediately along with Kaye in tow, marched down the hall to the living room to see who had snuck onto our premises.

When we got there, there was no one in sight. Kaye assured me that there was indeed an elderly man sitting in that chair reading a newspaper. I was not doubting her since I'd been experiencing similar sightings. So I asked her to describe him, his build, his look, and his dress. I know she thought that odd, but what have I got to lose. I didn't want to frighten the child, so I was playing it as if I knew who he was.

Her description was as follows: A plaid, long sleeve shirt, work pants, (not blue jeans), lace up work shoes, and he had a full head of hair that was grey. He was slim, not overweight, and was old, like a grandfather would look.

What she described was exactly the same man I'd seen several times myself.   So, I thanked her. She seemed satisfied and went off to find what the rest of the crew were up to outside.

Now, comes into this story the 'piece of resistance'   Our next door neighbor Pearl, along with her cousin, Ruth, just happened to stop by one day for a visit months after a number of these episodes took place. Our conversations went in many different directions and ended up talking about how we'd really made a lot of improvements on the property and house. I was telling them some of the obstacles we'd run into by first having to shovel garbage out of the rooms and attic. We had emptied out wheelbarrows full, not only of old clothes and cans of food that were blown out from spoilage, but the roof on the house had been cedar shakes at one time. All that material had been left in the attic when they put on the tin roof. The place had really been neglected.

Pearl, having lived here her entire life, began telling me how the previous owner had let it go to pot after his wife had passed. And that had been years. So, now I guess I could understand how canned goods had been neglected along with everything else. I reckon the man had just given up and did just enough to keep him going.

She then told me how she was the one who discovered the previous owners' body sitting propped up by a fence post, between the house and the barn. It was a somewhat dirt road that connected the two. I exclaimed that I didn't know he had actually passed while on the property. She didn't know if that made any difference to us or not, but the owner before him has also passed on this property.

What happens next is the clincher. For some unknown reason, Pearl described to me, in detail, how she discovered the last owner's body, down to exactly what he was wearing. You guessed it; plaid shirt, long sleeves, work pants, and laced up work shoes.

Well, I had nothing at this point to lose, except friendship with a neighbor and her cousin, and gossip throughout the entire town. So I just jumped in with both feet and hoped for the best outcome. I guess you can say that you will never know what people believe unless you ask them. To my surprise, both women believed in the afterlife, spirits, and experiences of the unknown realm. They both truly believed that the deceased man was still living or visiting his home. We had the best discussion and tried to figure out how to send him on his way. After all, he was dead. Why hang around here?

Here I'm going to say that I was an infant in all this stuff. I was looking for answers and most of all help to rid our house of what had been happening up to that point and as you'll will learn, future events. None of us three had a clue, except just to pray. I'd already been doing that and having two more to join me seemed reasonable; strength in numbers and all that. So, needless to say now looking back, it didn't quite work out.

CHAPTER 7

Don, my husband, worked the third shift at the factory in town. For me, it wasn't so devastating, but he hated it. Couldn't get much done around the house or even go anywhere, since he slept most of the day. If we did go and do anything, there was a risk of him being so tired, he could harm himself at work or even fall asleep at the wheel coming home. So, there we were

The kids were in school. So by the time Don got home, most of the time, they were already gone. He rarely sat around, or even ate when the kids first got up. He usually would just hop right into bed. So, since I loved to sleep, after I got the kids off on the bus, I'd venture back to bed for a couple more hours. More than a few time though, Don would be a little late coming home and the kids were already be gone.

This particular morning was one of the times that the kids were already off to school. Don worked a little overtime and was not home yet, so I went ahead and headed back in bed. Just to let you know how some mornings played out under these circumstance, When Don finally would get

51

home, and I haven't quite gotten to sleep yet, I'd play possum. That, for some of you readers who have never lived or understand about living in a rural setting, has a meaning of playing like your asleep. It's like playing like your dead or being deceitful about something.

Possums have no line of defense (unless your close enough and they do have sharp teeth and will bite). So, in order to deceive their opponent, they play dead. Weird, huh?

Back to the story. So, I'd play like I was asleep, and when Don would come in, well, that's about as far as I'm willing to take this story.

So, I was still awake, lying there just daydreaming, with my eyes closed and savoring the quiet moment. That's when I heard footsteps coming down our hall. Let me explain how you could hear so clearly in this house.

This house was a little over 100 years old. When we bought our property, this old farm house was halfway sitting on the ground, literally. And what wasn't on the ground, was sitting on large (or I should say huge) stones stacked one on top of the other. A wisteria vine was growing into the back side of the wall next to the driveway. Most of the porches were just about gone. And it had three porches. The windows were in disarray. It's amazing the wood they used on these windows, must have been redwood. It wasn't rotten, just needed re-glazing and plenty of paint. They were the type of window you could open from either direction.

Remember, there was no air conditioning back in those days. So ventilation was a necessity. There was, once upon a time, rope with weights attached to each side of the casing frame to allow them to glide smoothly up and down.

The exterior was clapboard and from the front you'd think it was a well to do house. There still was fancy gingerbread scrolls on each turned post on the porch. Amazing that it was the one thing still intact. The front door was solid with a large window in the upper half that was now covered with a piece of plywood. I did design a stain glass and had it installed. It was a real eye catcher. The doorbell was built into the middle of the door. It was brass, with a knob and a turnkey. When you rang it, most of the time you could hear it throughout the house. But, rarely did anyone ever use it. Guess no one nowadays, knew what it was.

The front of the house had a bay window in the living room. It was what formed the shape of the right hand section of the house. There were huge windows on each of the three sections forming this bay. The fourth window, along with the two other windows which faced the front porch went all the way to the floor making those nine feet in height. One could open the window, duck, and pass from inside to outside with ease. Then there was a fifth window facing the side yard. Looked real pretty and was great in the summer. But come winter, and since the house faced the north, there just was not any use in attempting to heat that room. So during the winter months, that room remained shut. Those other two windows of the nine feet height, was our bedroom. The porch went from that living room, crossing over to the corner of the house. Since I disclosed that those windows were nine feet tall, that would make the ceilings throughout the house eleven feet in height.

As you walked into the front door, the front hall was eight feet wide and fifteen feet long. Some hall, huh? In some houses, that could be a living room or a bedroom. But wait... This was an old farmhouse dubbed fancy by the fancy scrolls on the front of it. So in essence, that was mainly the main part of the house that served as a breezeway during the summer months to help cool the rooms.

The room behind the living room was another bedroom. It had two doors to go into it.

One was off the front hall and another to go out to what use to be a wraparound porch. Yep, you heard me right; you'd have to go outside to go to the dining room which was behind the second bedroom, and the kitchen which was next in line. That made this back hall thirty five feet long. Imagine a hall measuring fifty-five feet in length.

Sometime in the past, and I don't know who actually did it, a previous owner had taken in this back porch and enclosed it making the only bathroom we had, a walk-in closet, and a large room. They had not done such a hot job on the structure. There was clapboard only half way up. The rest was windows just nailed up there. No casing to even consider. They had placed two doors, one coming out the side and another going out the back to another part of the same porch. I learned from a neighbor that the so called walk in closet used to be the bedroom of the Brantley's mother, until she had passed. OK.

The majority of the floors were heartwood pine. No subflooring. And they were halfway painted. Back in old days, people would buy a sheet of linoleum that looked like carpet and place it in the center of the floor. Then, they'd paint the floor with this god awful tan-ish, orange color the rest of the space. So, when you took up the old linoleum, there was the original, none stained or painted, wood. Having no subflooring meant wind could blow through the cracks. I asked my father-in-law why they were built that way. He explained that they'd take a bucket, soap, and a mop or brush; they'd throw water on the floor, scrub the floors, and then mop up the dirty water. Hum? I guess that's one way of keeping a clean floor. So oak flooring wasn't a good idea for that type of flooring in an old farmhouse. And the paint helped preserve the wood, plus he said, looked neater.

Now that you have a somewhat picture of what we were living in, you can possible understand how that when anyone walked in this house, you could hear it plain as day.

Have you ever noticed, --maybe not-- how each individual has a certain stride to their walk? I could tell which of my children were walking in the house. Weight played a big part into it, along with their stride.

So, while I was playing possum in our bed, I heard Don walking the length of the hall. This would be from the back door, almost the full forty feet length, to our bedroom door. I looked at the clock and wondered what he was doing home so early? Well, just maybe, the factory had runout of parts and they let them go home early. That had happened a few time in the past. So I roll over on my side and pull the covers partly over my face so in case I smile, he won't see me. My top leg is bent and the one on the bottom is stretched out straight.

When the footsteps stopped, I waited for the next move. A hand went on the right side of my stretched out leg and another one on the left side. Then there was a gentle push. We had a full waterbed. This was not the kind of mattress that had baffles built within it. So any slight move, and you were being rocked. The water in the bed was misplaced slightly causing a small roll. I waited, nothing was said, and it happened again. Moments passed and it happened a third time. By that time, I was going to give up my ruse. I spoke and said something to the effect, 'Okay, okay. I'm awake'.

Complete silence.

I got this real creepy feeling. Moments ticked by, seeming like an eternity with nothing else taking place. There were no more shoves on the bed, no more footsteps, yet the feeling of hands pressing down on either side of my leg was still present.

What to do? I was really having strange sensations now, BIG TIME. So, I decided to sit up as fast as I could and face the foot of the bed.

I did it, but when I looked at the area, there was absolutely nothing, no one, nowhere, empty space. ?!?!#**?!?!

What the (blank) was going on? I heard Don's distinct footsteps walk the entire length of our hall. I heard him walk into our bedroom and stop at the foot of the bed. I felt him shove on the waterbed not once, but several times. The bed had floated up and down as a waterbed would. But, yet, there is no one in this room.

After a moment of getting over the shock of not seeing my husband, or anyone else as a matter of fact, I vacate the bed and go to investigate. Not really knowing if I'd run into anyone or anything, I'm really scared. The hair all over my body is standing at attention and I am glad is it daylight.

I'm calling out Don's name and also saying,

'Okay, this is not funny. Quit playing games with me." But still, total silence.

I go looking through the house. I peer down the hall. Nothing. I cross over to the living room. Nothing. I go to our daughters bedroom. Nothing. After going through the bathroom, our son's room, and the kitchen, still no one. Mind you, while I am doing this, I am also looking under the beds, behind the couch, behind the curtains, everywhere anyone could slip behind or under to hide.

Finally, I look outside from the back part of the hall, where everyone parked their vehicles. Don's truck was nowhere to be found. Then I get this bright idea that maybe it was an intruder. So I check all those large windows. In a way, that would be stupid since we had all of them nailed shut along with a stick propped up in them so they couldn't be pushed open. And of course, they were still all secure. So, last but not least, I check the doors. The back door coming into the hall, the side door coming into the kitchen, the front door, and the last door coming into the side of the back hall, were all locked. I mean, I would have seen or heard someone coming into the front door since it was within view of our bed. And plus, I heard Don's footsteps entering our bedroom all the way down that long hall. I was frightened, and it really set in when I saw that the back porch door was not only locked, but we had a screen door that was latched. Don would have to knock for me to let him in.

While I'm trying to contemplate what next to do, I see Don pulling up the driveway and parking. I immediately go unlock the back door to meet him.

When he gets up in the porch, he realizes something is wrong with me. I begin accusing him of pulling a prank, and saying that this is not funny. Of course, he has no idea why I'm so upset.

So I begin explaining how my morning went after getting the kids off to school. That's when He gets alarmed. He has me stand on the back porch while he investigates. He goes from room to room looking as I had done previously, to see if anyone broke in and was hiding. Nothing.

So then, he calls our neighbor across the street. Our house is a slight bit lower in elevation than theirs is. So they can see everything going on at our place if they wished to. Funny, I believe they wished to because once the lady of the house made a comment to us how she kept a pair of binoculars at her door (which faced our house) if she needed to see something closer. Hum?

The couple told Don, 'No, as far as they knew, no one came or went out of our driveway that morning. (except when Don arrived)'.

So, what do you think he did next, to my argument? He calls the sheriff's department and tells them. By this time, I'm convinced it wasn't a real person. With all that had been happening in this house thus far, it was one of the poltergeists having some fun with me, at my expense.

Well, the sheriff comes out. Don explains to him what took place. The sheriff does not take it seriously. I just can't tell him the doors were all locked. I did not want to be known as a basket case, a nut, hearing things, whatever you want to call me. This county is small. Word spreads. I had two kids in school. I didn't want repercussions of any incident here to affect my children, much less me. So, being the good ole boy network here, the sheriff and my husband just chew the fat while in our driveway and then he leaves.

Don said if it happened again, call them and they would investigate more thoroughly next time. Good. Maybe it'll all eventually just go away.

Right. Fat chance. But I can wish and dream can't I?

My Grandmother's Portrait

The Old Yellow House

CHAPTER 8

Now there was one entity that seemed to want to play tricks, or mind games. I believe it is what is called a poltergeist. For those who do not know what this is or have never heard of such a thing, I'm going to quote a wonderful definition from GAIA.com's explanation:

"Poltergeists are centered on one person known as the epicenter. The epicenter is typically an adolescent going through puberty or adolescents going through a lot of emotional distress. Once an epicenter releases a vast amount of negative emotions, a poltergeist can form from the epicenters kinetic energy.

Another instance can occur if a spirit feeds on to this negative energy and becomes poltergeist-like entities. There have been instances of older adults as epicenters where poltergeists form out of repressed memories, financial problems, marital problems or other instances.

A poltergeist activity can range from subtle knockings to, on rare occasions, throwing objects at the epicenter or anyone else. The most common occurrences from poltergeists are moving objects on their own, whether it is moving keys to the fridge or quickly moving heavy furniture or appliances around. This activity only occurs when the epicenter is present."

What I'm about to write about is what happened to our son. As far as I know, this didn't have anything to do with the man a few of us were seeing. This spirit was a mischievous one. I'll explain several instances which happened during the night.

Brad's room was towards the back of the house, off from that long hall that went through the center of the house and right off the kitchen. There were two doors going into his room and a large window that looked out to the side yard and a porch.

This once served as a dining room. Since we needed another bedroom, and the house had such large rooms, this was changed into his room and dining room table ended up in that huge hall. That is why this room had two doors, one out into the hall and the other opened into the kitchen.

All this had to be explained so you'd understand what I'm about to tell you. More than once, did my son have this happen to him, amongst other things.

Brad is an extremely sound sleeper. It takes a lot just to wake him up. I know he really appreciates me writing this about him, but it is the truth. And this must be told in order to understand his experience. In other words, it really takes something to wake this kid up.

There he is, sound asleep in his bed. He is awakened (which in itself is a miracle) by the rattling of dishes. This just happened to be the middle of the night. So, as he described to me, he could not figure out why I would be in the kitchen, cleaning out the cabinets and rearranging the dishes.

He gets out of bed, looks into the kitchen, and sees all the kitchen cabinet doors open, and every dish, glass, pot, and pan, laid out on every available surface. I am nowhere in sight.

He thinks, 'Hum? Now that's strange. Where did mom go and why is she doing this in the middle of the night?'

On this note, he goes through the house to investigate. When he finds me and his father sound asleep in our own beds, with the same as his sister asleep in her bed, he is dumb founded. So, he returns to his own room, without waking anyone, and goes back to his bed.

Sound asleep a second time that same night, he is again awakened by the same rattling of dishes, pots, and pans. He gets out of bed again to investigate. Looking into the kitchen once more, all the dishes are back in the cabinets with all the doors closed. The kitchen is back as it was before all this happened.

After all of us got up that next morning, Brad told us of the events of the night. Of course, we believed him after what had been taking place to us personally. But never had a poltergeist exhibited such a dramatic exposure. This happened more than once to him.

Years before we ever moved to Mississippi, my husband had gotten into doing magic. Some of the tricks and props he had made himself, while others he had purchased. At one time, a magician was selling out his entire act and quitting the business. So, the deal was to purchase all or nothing. No breaking up any part of his collection. My husband brought home this collection and sold off parts of it since a lot of the acts he already owned. Along with this collection, he acquired a ventriloquist dummy with case. Now magic was one thing, but a dummy was not something he cared to put into his act. So away it went into the back of the closet.

Once we moved to Tyro, items got placed throughout the house differently than they had in our previous location. This old house had only two closets, if one would really call them a closet. They were so narrow, a clothes hanger wouldn't fit into them. I found out later that the reason houses built back then had no closets was due to taxes. They appraised property and houses by acreage, timber, size of house, construction, outbuildings, and how many closets were in your house. That is where wardrobes and armoires came into being.

That said, there was no out of sight storage in this old house. So the ventriloquist dummy ended up in, you guessed it, Brad's room. It was a joke amongst the 'guys' Brad hung out with. They'd get him out and play, as kids would, making his mouth and arms move. Then they'd just shove him in the corner. Brad never did care for this 'thing' and neither did I. It just for some reason, gave us the creeps. And it did look creepy with that glued hair, fat lips, and suit. It looked almost clownish, but yet similar to those dummies you see on the old Twilight shows. Now, you get my drift.

Needless to say, with everything we were experiencing in and around that old house, you can just guess what's about to happen next. Yes, the dummy started to come to life.

Frozen with fear, Brad let it be known, he wanted that thing gone. Not only out of his room, but gone from the house. I was only too pleased to finally get that thing away from us. My husband placed all the magic he had, including the dummy, for sale and got rid of it all. I have no idea if the man had any experiences happen to him that we had bought it from, but getting into magic does open a door for some who have no idea what's on the other side.

I just say, good riddance.

Brad had a set of bunk beds in his room. He liked to sleep on the top bunk. So when his friends spent the night, they naturally would be on the bottom bunk.

As before, this next set of experiences happened more than once. It was the same thing that was happening to me, but not on the same nights.

Most of the times this took place, someone was spending the night with Brad. Were 'they' trying to prove that no matter the circumstances, 'they' could appear and stifle you? I do not have an answer for that since it happened also to me with Don lying right next to me in bed.

What was going on, many call sleep paralysis. I've heard shows where people tell their theory of what they felt it was. For Brad and me, what we felt was some heavy object or thing pressing down on our entire body to where we couldn't budge an inch. We couldn't even open our mouths to cry out. Our eyes could move. Our brains could think. It was so devastating that it woke us from a sound sleep. Our brains were screaming, 'let me go!' And yet, the person in the room with us, never knew anything was going on. The one thing I felt and Brad felt during and after these episode was fear. Fear of not ever being able to move again. Fear of the heavy weight on us. Fear of the invisible. Fear of it happening again (which it did). And you know, fear does paralyze us. We each experienced this first hand more times than we care to.

CHAPTER 9

You'd think that with all the activity going on and in around his old yellow house, that 'ghosts' would not be exposing themselves. Plus, we never knew when their appearances would happen. It never made any difference if you were alone or with many people around, the only time we all experienced a phenomenon were the cold spots in the kitchen. Other times, only one individual would see or experience their presence.

One night everyone was in bed asleep. I'm usually a sound sleeper, but for unknown reasons this night, I woke up. Lying there, I imagined a presence standing at the foot of our bed. I felt pressure next to my outstretched leg. Then I felt the same pressure on the other side of that same leg. Remember, we had a waterbed. Then as if someone or something decided to go further onto the bed, the first pressure moved up about eighteen inches beside my leg. I felt as if someone was getting into the bed with us.

Startled by these moves, I immediately sat upright in order to confront whatever or whoever it happened to be. I was scared out of my wits.

There was absolutely nothing there. The pressure on both sides of my leg had lifted. And to top it all off, Don never woke up. I'm so frightened I'm now shaking and can hardly breathe. I don't remember going back to sleep.

     Another experience I had was what I've heard some people call 'sleep paralysis'. There are many theories out there as to what causes this. Many people have made the assumption about alien abduction. For me, I know that that is not the case. All I know is that I'd wake up not being able to move, breath, or even cry out. It felt like something had its hand over my mouth. Plus, I felt as if a heavy weight was laying on top of my entire body. After much struggling in my mind and screaming out (in my mind), it would finally lift. Catching my breath, I look over at my husband and there he is, sound asleep not realizing the turmoil I was in. How could this be happening to me and no one else knows, especially being within arm's length?

Many times upon retiring to bed, I'd no sooner get to bed and there would be music playing. One of the doors across from our bedroom door is where our daughter's bedroom was. Remember, she had two doors in her room; one in the front hall and the second opening up into what we dubbed the back hall which use to be a porch. We had gotten her a pretty good stereo one year for Christmas. Her collection of cassettes was a fairly good one of 80's music. She'd sit in her room and play album after album as most young teens would do. When it came time for bed, all music was to be turned off.

So, when I heard music playing, I was mad. I'd have to get out of bed, go across that eight foot wide hall enter her room to tell her to turn it off. To my surprise, as I got half way across the hall, the music would cease playing. I'd stop, turn my head to listen, then proceed into her room.

There'd she be in bed, sound asleep. No sign of any quick escape from turning the stereo off and jumping back into bed. Her room was rather large and remember, anyone walking on those floors could be heard.

This puzzling incident happened to me time and time again over the course of a year. I'd ask her about it and she promised she never listened to her stereo once everyone was in bed. I have to believe her because it seems reasonable that if she were playing her music after bedtime, I'd at least catch her red handed eventually. Oh, by the way, this was before remote controls, just in case you might be thinking she had one hid under her pillow.

_____

_____

There was one young man my son met at school that he clicked with. Both had a love for the outdoors and both loved adventurous exploring. What I found out years later into what they had experienced and got into, is enough to send a mom through the roof. I'll just say that it's a good thing I knew nothing of their escapades back then, or I would have locked Brad in his room and thrown away the key, until he turned eighteen, better yet twenty-one years old.

There was a joke amongst my family I'd like to share. I didn't think it was funny, but everyone else did. It all began with me shopping at the Tuesday Morning store in Memphis, Tennessee off of Hacks Cross road. We bought a lot of items for our house there and one item I was intrigued with was this depiction made out of cloth of a hot air balloon. I know it doesn't sound like much, but I love to look at them. It was purely decorative and a little pricey for our budget. Since I sewed, I knew I could come up with enough scraps to make me one and hang it in one of our rooms. So, I sketched it, while there, in the store so I wouldn't have to put every detail to memory and went home and began this project. This was long before smart phone with cameras.

I actually made two hot air balloons, one for me and one for my daughter. In order for them to be "blown up", I found balloons large enough to place up into the top part and then blew it up to form the upper shape. I had mine hanging from the ceiling in the living room. So proud was I of my creations.

The joke I started out to describe was, every time this buddy of Brad's would come over, and walk into our living room, my balloon in the decoration would burst. The first time this happened, I didn't think much of it. I had plenty of spare balloons. The second time, I was thinking, "Hum". The third time is when it was getting ridiculous. That is when my family started making the joke, "Don't let him in the house, he'll burst mom's balloon". The young man really didn't know what he was doing. He never gave it a second thought. It was us who were thinking about what was 'attached' to him to cause this phenomenal episode to take place. I finally had to move my balloon into my bedroom just to keep it safe. To this day, since moving it, my balloon still remains full. Oh, did I mention it has been over twenty years? Yea, exactly my thought, too.

There's another incident that happened to my husband and myself which involved this young man. Brad had already moved away from home. This young man came by to ask if he could hunt on our place. We do not give permission to hunt. But, people will still hope to gain access regardless.

My husband and he stood on the front porch talking for a good while. He never stepped one foot in doors. After they finished and he had left, I began having excruciating pains in my hip joints. Don had the same, but only in his shoulder joints. This happened on a Saturday evening. That night, neither one of us got much sleep if any at all. Sunday was no better. We did everything we could think of to alleviate the pain. I was even thinking of how I'd be able to function the rest of my life with such pain. Don was no better. I couldn't sit, couldn't stand, couldn't lay on either my right side or left side. No position would relieve this pain. So Sunday night was no better than Saturday night.

Don had to go to work Monday morning. He was wondering how he would operate with such pain. So he informed me that if it became impossible to do his job, he'd check out and come back home.

With all that said and with all the pain we were in, I was past the point of being desperate. We had both prayed for each other and ourselves to no avail. But now, I was on the warpath. I stood in the middle of our living room and commanded that whatever and wherever this 'thing' had come from leave "NOW".

It was about 10:00 in the morning. I immediately had total relief. The phone rings. It's Don.

"Guess what," he says, "the pain in my shoulders left just a few minutes ago."

I told him we'd talk when he got home. So, the only explanation to these happenings had to be through this same young man. What was following and/or attached to him that caused such havoc in our lives? Many incidents seemed to happen to him I will not go into, so it was not only us this was happening to. Supernatural phenomenon's are like guessing games. We can come up with many theories, but that is about as far as it can take us. Your guess is as good as mine.

CHAPTER 10

Now let me try to recreate the one paranormal incident that my daughter and her friends, Linda and Danny experienced. With all the occurrences my son and I were having, Linell only had this happen to her. She can't remember how many times she had it, but it was only through this medium that the paranormal exposed itself to her. I'm speaking here of the Ouija Board.

How or why I still had this game, is beyond my comprehension. I look back and wonder why I was still toting this thing from house to house as we moved. But, here it was and now it surfaced. Where I came across it, I haven't a clue. But when it appeared, she began asking about it.

I told her the crux of what I had experienced, but yet through my ignorance and stupidity, I allowed her to mess with it along with her friends. I don't know if anyone realizes it or maybe they do, but one person alone can operate the planchette.

Most nights during the summer, the neighborhood was alive way past dark. Many kids lived in our little community and they'd ride bikes to each other's homes and a lot of the times small tents would be set up in our backyards where they'd all be sleeping over. It brought back memories when I watched the Netflix show "Stranger Things"; not of the monsters, but the way the kids all hung out. That is what I speak of when I say the kids were out having a good time.

On one particular night, Linell had her friend, Linda, over spending the night. Danny, the older brother of Chuck, Brad's friend from around the corner, came by to see what everyone was doing. Like most young teens, they wanted to have fun, occupy their time with a game or such. So Linell told them of the newly discovered Ouija Board.

They hemmed and hawed, going back and forth jesting that it wasn't real and would never work. But, with nothing else to do, why not try it out.

Well, the ambience had to be set. They set throughout the house to look for candles, music to play in the background, and closing the curtains to the bedroom. With the stage set, they began reading the instructions that came with the board.

Okay, all lights out and only candles burning, they set out to ask it questions. They first introduced themselves to the board. Then came the wait to see if it would respond. All fingertips were lightly placed upon the planchette. At first, like most experiences, nothing happened. Time passed, nervous laughter and discussion about the board would occasionally erupt. Waiting seemed endless. But then finally, a little budge happened. Of course, each teen accused the others of moving it, and of course, each one denied that they had. And yet now, the planchette really began to stir, moving inches to and fro, across the board.

The instructions were to either ask a question with a yes or no answer, or to allow the board to tell what entity had shown up to speak to the participants.

Dealing with this phenomenal experience for the first time, they decided to see what the Board had to tell them. Three messages came forth.

The first was a killing that had taken place in an alley in New York City. The event had something to do with the black market and the person had been shot and killed by a 357 revolver.

The second was a child speaking to them through the Board. At this writing, none of those present could remember any more than that of the second message except that he or she was fourteen years old when they died.

By this time, the teens were scared, but also excited that maybe this thing really did work. Yet, they each accused the others of pushing the planchette across the board, and making up stories.

For the third message, they decided to ask a more personal question. Why they chose this question is beyond me, but ask they did.

This old yellow house was on the market. We had had enough of the episodes to last a lifetime. We were trying to sell it along with around five acres to sweeten the deal. We planned on building a home on the remainder of our acreage. So with that in mind, they wanted to see if and when the house would sell.

The entity working the planchette told them yes, it would sell and that it would be in August. I'll tell you now that August came and went and it did not sell. So, our contract ran out not too long after that with the realtor. But wait --- the teens didn't ask in what year it would sell. That following spring, we put it back on the market and low and behold, it sold. And you've probably guessed right, it was in August. Go figure. Is this real? Is it not? I don't have a clue. You can make up your own mind.

Now comes the turning point of the night. Still accusing each other of helping the planchette along and making up stories to scare the others, they agree to take their hands off of the device and see what happens then. With that accomplished, you know that planchette still moved across that board on its own! Well Danny freaks; jumps up, accusing the girls of being witches or something; and then he straightway runs home.

I know it is not funny, but I bet there was lightning streaks following him all the way home; you know, the kind you see in the TV cartoons? I don't blame him. Remembering the experience my friend and I had had years ago, we did the same running out of the house. To this day, Danny still speaks of that experience with fear in his voice. Something was up and he didn't want any part of it ever again.

After I found out what had transpired with that game --again -- our family went through our home and collected any item that we felt was holding any evil enchantments, magic, sorcery, charms, etc. Even if we were unsure, we still gathered it. We then had us a bonfire and burned all of it. The kids in the neighborhood thought we were off our rocker. But with all the stuff happening, we didn't care how they felt. We wanted it out.

CHAPTER 11

It has now been decades since we lived in that old yellow house. A lot has transpired since, in both our lives, with understanding, and finally with the climax of the house.

After we sold the house, I rarely visited the new tenants. This may sound weird, but, I was afraid what was living mostly unseen there, just might follow me back to my new dwelling. After all, we were still on the same acreage that once was one piece of real estate. Call me superstitious, I don't care. I was taking no chances.

We actually met all the new tenants, owners over a period of time, and not one of them ever voiced any strange goings on in that place. Or maybe, some are not quite as sensitive or pay any attention to mishaps. Who knows? Either way, I just stayed clear of the dwelling.

The couple that bought it from us was from Raleigh, the northern section of Memphis, Tennessee. They were a little older than us, already having grandchildren. She was used to being active in their community, but wanted property to retire on when that day would finally arrive for them, which would have been just a few years down the road. But, being miles away from her club gatherings or get-togethers eventually took its toll on their social lives, and they sold the house and moved back to the city.

She was a follower of the New Age movement at that time and had the opposite beliefs that seemed to be traveling in on my quest. We never really got into a big discussion on the unseen realm. Though it does make me wonder if she relished any connection that might have occurred in that house.

The next couple who purchased the house seemed to just use it as a stepping stone to their next property. He worked and she was in college. Rarely were they ever seen out in the yard. Mostly it was just a place to sleep, eat, and go. They never mingled with the neighbors. I'm not suggesting this was strange or even bad. I'm just saying that as soon as she graduated, they were gone, house sold. Oh, and I forgot to mention, with them rarely there, and with dogs in the house most of the day, the house was going down, physically. There was a lot of work now needed to bring it back to livable standards.

The third family who bought the house had children. They seemed to have grand plans of restoration when I first met them. The wife asked me if I'd come over and give her advice on what needed to be done since we were the ones who had initiated the past restoration. When I entered that house, reluctantly, I get a look at how the past occupants had lived. The whole place was a disaster, in my book. Compared to how we first saw the house and then restored it and what it had been allowed to degrade into, was heartbreaking. With all the work we had done, and then the finishing touches the couple behind us had accomplished, the place was a disaster. There were even holes in the floors where you could see the ground. And I mean holes, where a person could fit through. I couldn't see pouring any more money into this place. Most the windows needed to be replaced and at that size, it would cost a fortune.

Well, needless to say, they didn't last long in that place either. They couldn't find a buyer for what was owed on the property, so it went into disarray. Long story short, it went up for property taxes on the courthouse steps. By this time, vandals had a heyday. People came and went ripping pipes, porches, doors, you name it, off and out of that house. I actually watched as strangers pulled up to it and ripped it apart, piece by piece. I often wonder if any spirits attached itself to those items and followed them home? For that reason alone, I stayed clear.

Eventually, some kids decided one night, to have fun. They spray painted words that I will not repeat, boldly, all around the house. What a sight to see when you drove down the road. Well, the new owners now thought enough was enough. They commissioned our local volunteer fire department to have a practice fire. They burnt it to the ground. Now, there is nothing left of that house. Only photos I have and memories, if you want to call it that.

BUT WAIT!

THE STORY DOESN'T END HERE:

Across the street from the once existing old yellow house are two homes. Neither one has the original occupants, being that they have all passed on. So, new families have moved into both houses

(not at the same exact time, but over the past several years.)

We've met and spoken to one particular family whose driveway is almost exactly lined up with the old yellow houses driveway. Both pieces of property sits up on a hill with the road looking as though it had been bulldozed through the incline making it relatively flat and the house up. So, when you're at either one of the houses front yards, you are looking across as if on the same level.

As I wrote earlier, I would have liked to have had several items from that old house, but was always concerned if spirits could attach themselves to said articles and come home with me. So, I passed up any temptations to even wander into the house once it was not occupied and as people were coming and going ripping the house apart.

With all that said, one day Don stopped to speak to that neighbor across the street. He mentioned that I was attempting to write a book about the experiences we had while living in that old yellow house. Upon hearing about just a few incidents in minor details, Bob (the neighbor) began telling him of events taken place within his house.

After Don got home and told me what Bob had said, I just had to speak to him myself to see what was transpiring. I know the family that had actually built that house long before we even moved to Tyro. They raised two girls there who were slightly younger than myself. Both were married and had families of their own. The father died before the wife did. She stayed in the house, not wanting to leave it. Not until her youngest daughter demanded she moved in with her, so she could keep an eye on her mother, did any other family ever occupy their house. The house then sat empty for a while before it was finally sold. So, Bob and his family were only the second couple to ever occupy that house.

The expression on Bob's face when I asked him if he would share with me what he and his family experienced in their home, was that of pure fear. While he told of the story of events, he confessed that hair on his arms was standing up. I could tell he was freaked just by the tone of his voice. It was of shear dread and terror as he spoke. The man truly didn't like what was happening and quite didn't understand from where or why it was all taking place. I also need to mention that others staying or visiting his home, also experienced the unexplained happenings too.

So what was taking place? I asked him if I could have his permission to write about it and he said yes. I did change his name though.

It all began with the pictures on the walls. Their hall was a short one compared to what that old yellow house had. Their photos, like most, were framed, behind glass. There is a large frame that is solid, with a matt and slots cut into it to form a decoupage that hung on one end of their hall. Other single pictures were also on the hall walls. This one decoupage frame was rather large.

Coming home from work and school (they have a child) one day, upon entering the hall, all ---- and I do mean all ------- of the photos were lying face down on the floor just as if someone placed them there. Okay? How did this happen? Questions were asked of each other, with all confessing that they never touched the pictures. And on top of that, why would they lay them face down on the hall floor? With no explanation, they hung all the pictures back up.

It wasn't too long after this, that it happened again. Still, no explanation. But then a stranger incident occurred. While in the house, a noise of broken glass came from this same hall. Rushing there to see what all the commotion was about and upon arrival, that same large frame had slammed into the opposite wall (end upon end) and had shattered, laying now on the floor.

The family also would come home finding all the photos in the house lying face down where ever they sat. (as on a shelf or table).

Then after this freakiness, another strange thing began to take place. This family only had one child, a boy, who was of elementary school age. I need to place here in the story, that there are no babies in our neighborhood. I don't really know of anyone who even has grandchildren of such a young age of infancy. With that said, Bob and his family began to hear a baby cry.

Shocked, they went around the house looking from room to room as to where this crying could be coming from. They came up empty handed and yet, the crying was consistent. Next, they wandered outside still looking to see where this crying was originating from. And still, nothing. It wasn't outdoors, but seemed to be within their dwelling. Then it ceased. Okay, what and why is this taking place after having photos smash to the floor?

This phenomenon went on over a period of weeks, on not any particular day or time. Not keeping score, but it seems it happened at least 6 more times. Then it ceased, which in their book, was a relief. But now, why and how is this happening?

On another occasion, Bob was home alone. You may know how it is when alone, not expecting any loud noise to occur and if or when it does, you jump 'out of your skin'? Well, there he was, minding his own business, when a door slams shut. There was no explaining this by a draft or any window being open since all were shut. It had never happened before and they'd been in this house now for years. He investigates, finds the door and opens it, looking through the house and calling to make sure no one other than himself was home. Alone, he goes back to his business at hand. Again, the same door slams. Now, he's really spooked. He goes back and opens it a second time. It happens once again. He decides this time to leave it shut.

Bob said he was an extremely heavy sleeper as where his wife sleeps very light, waking to the slightest noise. He explained why he was telling me this. It really takes a lot to wake him from a sound sleep.

Well, one night while asleep in bed, he was awakened by someone running in his 'short' hall. His wife was already awake lying there wondering what the heck was going on. Sitting up, they went to investigate thinking it was their son playing a prank. (in the middle of the night?) They discovered, he was in his bed sound asleep, for real. So, not waking him, they returned to their bed. No sooner had they pulled the covers up, that the running began again. Bob jumps up and peers down the hall. Nobody was present. Now mind you, it would only take a 5 step run, one way, in that hall. And Bod said it was running back and forth, back, and forth. No explanation for this occurrence.

By this time of presenting what facts have occurred in his home, Bob was pretty shaken. He had two fellows there at his home helping him around the yard. (we were standing outside as he spoke to me of the events). They were corroborating all he was speaking of and then added, tell her about your vacation and your sister.

Well, his family took a vacation. They asked his sister to house sit for them. She agreed and off they went. After just several days, they get a phone call. The sister is freaking and saying abnormal incidents are happening, plus, she feels as if someone was watching her all the time. So, she left.

Other occurrences may have taken place. But, with all this happening, I explained to him some of my family's events in the house that use to be directly across the street from him. I then explained to him what a poltergeist was. I was sorry to hear that he was having this sort of trouble, but there was one question I just had to ask:

"Think back," I asked. "When did all of this begin? Was it while that old yellow house was standing, or after they burned it to the ground?"

Bob thought a moment, and then answered, "Now that you ask that question, you know, nothing ever happened while that house stood. It all began after it was destroyed and completely removed."

With amazement, we just stood there.

My question now remains; did the 'spirits, apparitions, spooks, poltergeist, whatever one wants to call them, wander across the street to another dwelling?

PART 2

THIS WORLD WE LIVE IN

CHAPTER 12

I never was what you'd call a religious person. All I remember when I was young is that I always believed in God. My parents never went to church or synagogue. But they instilled in my brother and myself a standard of morals and ways. It, for me, was an excellent foundation which I later passed on to my children. Some may call it living by the 'golden rule'. For us, it was just plain common sense. Do right, live right, treat people with respect, mind your manners and mind your own business. Work hard and you'll eventually be repaid for all that you accomplish. That's how I was raised.

The times I did go to church would be on the invite from my girlfriends. I wanted to be with them, so off to church my parents would let me go. You might know how it usually goes, with some churches, but eventually some men from the congregation would show up at your home for an invitation to attend their congregation. Then, to my parents surprise, they hit them up for contributions of tithes, since I was attending. I hadn't a clue what all this was about. I only knew that I wanted to be with my friends. Church politics was not on my list of having to know God and His ways. Eventually, I quit attending until after I was married.

When our children were born, I began attending church once again. I wanted them to be taught good standards and morals. They even attended a Christian school in the beginning, before we eventually moved into that old yellow house. Needless to say, church attendance was sketchy.

Once we were in Tyro, and our lives were changed by the poltergeists, appearances, and such, the search was on for answers. But where to look? As in most communities, we had invites from a few of the denominations around us. We settled on the two in our neighborhood. I wrote earlier about the Baptist and Methodist congregation, so I will not repeat the schedule they had. So we just fell into step, whenever we did go. One thing I despise is when people put pressure on others to try to make them feel guilty for not showing up on a Sunday. What is that, peer pressure? Do they think you're going to hell for missing a meeting? And if you did decide one denomination suits you better than another, the evangelism is on. Like I mentioned earlier, I was raised to keep my nose out of others business. This tight knit community was an eye opener for us in more than just one way. Remember, most all of them were born and raised here. We were the outsiders.

Our children eventually got into many of the clubs offered in our area. Plus, in the summer, softball was king. We ran ourselves ragged between 4-H and Cub Scouts.

We were even leaders of a few troops and clubs. On top of that, I got involved in Tyro's Homemakers Club amongst a few other organizations. Then, during the school year, the women who were home and not holding an outside job, went to Como to a non-denominational Bible study once a week. I had been invited to attend by my neighbors. They assured me that it was on volunteer basis to answer any questions presented. They met all together at first, had announcements and prayer, and then went off to assigned rooms where, a leader would go over last week's handouts of questions to be discussed. By the end of seven years, an attendee would have read and studied the entire Bible.

Eventually I succumbed to their prodding and attended a meeting. It was always on a Thursday morning. Women from around the whole area attended and I kinda liked how it was set up. This program was, I found out later, called the

Explorers Club and was nationwide. And true to my neighbor's word, no one was ever called on. It was truly all voluntary. I was hooked. Even though I had attended church off and on for years, I never really understood the Bible. It always seems foreign to me. Now was my chance to dig in and dig in was exactly what I did.

While all this was happening to me with the Explorers Club, my house was giving me fits with the apparitions and poltergeists. Now you may assume that all my house problems was due to my attending a Bible study. But that just isn't true. The house episodes had come first. The Bible study in my mind, was going to be my answer.

Reading about God, Jesus, disciples, miracles, Satan, and demons, was what I felt I needed. The answer had to be in the Bible. Preachers in our churches, Sunday school teachers, and preachers on TV, spoke of casting out demons, commanding Satan to leave in Jesus' Name. All you needed was to believe and the devil had to vacate. Demons had to obey your every word. I mean, isn't that what it says and what preachers preach? I was hooked. If it said it in the Scriptures, then I was going to believe it along with other believers.

I took everything at face value as I studied. I mean, after-all, the preachers on Sunday morning were saying it from behind the pulpits. They were called by God to preach His word. They were held at a higher standard than just us congregants, right? So, with all the happenings in our home, off I went to meet with preachers for help. You can just imagine the reception I had. I was as a babe in the woods, innocent of understanding.

As I disclosed, to one preacher after another, the problem I was having, I innocently held back nothing until I'd see the shocked look on each face. Then I'd back off in puzzlement of why they were acting in such a way. After all, they preached casting out demons from behind the pulpit. Now was a chance for them to hone their skills. Didn't they believe they had the authority? I believed them at their word and God's Word. So, come over and help me. Show me how it's done. I'll supply the anointing oil or you can bring your special blend. What is it going to take to anoint my house and get rid of these hindrances?

Surprisingly or maybe not -- I had NO takers. It was as though they hit the door running. After all, who or what am I? Am I so special to have such attention in my life as a haunted house? I even had one preacher pat me on top of my head and exclaim, "There, there; your imagination has just run amuck with you."

Very rapidly, I was losing faith in 'men of the cloth.' Looks like if I wanted any peace the only one I could rely on was me, myself, and I. Skipping over a few years from this point, I eventually met some followers who believed as I was believing at that point of my life. And guess what? It just happened to be a group of women. Fancy that. It took women to stand up to the unseen and drive it out. So, at that stage of my life's journey,

I finally had found a niche. The women (and a few men) met in followers homes and also had meeting and Bible studies at a few churches during their off hours. And once a month, there would be special gatherings in conference rooms.

For me and my family, it was a dream come true, and breath of fresh air; others who truly believed and walked in the Word. The meeting we attended and the friendships we acquired were so precious to us. These were not phony. These people not only talked the talk, but walked it out with signs and wonders, and miracles. They traveled to different areas in the United States along with a few foreign countries, so we had a wealth of exposure to different cultures and beliefs. There was no playing games.

They were serious and yet a joy to be with. I learned a lot from these people. I also dug deep into the Scriptures, taking it all in from cover to cover. This studying of the Word became my obsession. Dealing with the apparitions and experiences I had and was having in my house, thrust me into what was prevalent in the area, and yes, country I lived in. That would, of course be Christianity.

I was led to look at the whole picture, more or less. I was trying to separate myself from what was seen and heard and attempting to look at this world as a whole picture. There were a lot of questions and I couldn't look at just one source.

So attempting to get to the root of the matter, I looked towards Judaism. After all, it is written that that is where it all began. My studies led me to the Torah, the first five books of the Bible. That seemed to be the foundation. I visited synagogues and found that they are as much chopped up in their beliefs as much as Christianity is with all their denominations. There's even Messianic Judaism; ones' who go by Judaism believing in Yeshua (Jesus). Talk about confusing. Which page can one base their trust and truth?

I even traveled to Israel to see where all this "religion" started. It was just myself, along with my daughter (who was then grown) and my best friend. We were free to do whatever we pleased to do. We had rented a car and drove all around, from Tel Aviv, through the Valley of Megiddo, to Tiberias on the Sea of Galilee, to Jerusalem. We walked where those who went before walked and saw so many sights and items we had only read about and saw pictures of.

By the way, for anyone who is familiar with north Mississippi, the Sea of Galilee was shocking to see! It's not even half the size of Sardis Lake! To me, it was small. How can they call it a sea? Even the land (Israel) is tiny. It was nothing to drive from border to border. That's what's so amazing; everyone wants a piece of that real estate and there's not much to want, size wise that is. Now, don't get mad at me for saying this. I'm just stating, Israel is small.

We did have a marvelous time and truly enjoyed ourselves.

Along with my studies I also was lead into the natural way of living. I'm not going to go into how I was raised or lived my life, but just to say we never really went in for taking medications. That led me into studying herbs and food. After all, doesn't the Bible say that the plants were given to us for the healing of our bodies?

So, while in my studies, I learned that our world consists of vibrations. I'm not a scientist and would never pretend to be one or as smart as one. But, I've been told that everything is held together by different frequencies, ie. vibrations. And in order to help heal your body back to health, you need to find what plant matches that vibrational frequency to bring it back to perfection. This is my simplistic explanation. How did I arrive at this conclusion? God spoke (vibration) and it came into being. That's why words can build up, or tear down; destroy or revive. Even light is informative since it carries a vibration. And in that vibration is information.

I studied that with that information flowing continuously is the glue that holds all together. It feeds our souls which is directed to our hearts. That is how intuition works.

Haven't you ever heard someone say that they have a feeling about a certain situation or person? That's not head knowledge. That comes from deep within your soul. It's only when we filter this knowledge through our minds, that we end up with the wrong ideology. This could be why our world has been in such chaos since the beginning of time; that is the Garden.

The true communication can be tapped into in minute pieces, scattered abroad. It's only when 'man' puts his ideals into place, that structured beliefs become programmed into areas, resulting in religions in which even they are fractured.

All these beliefs seem to be based in fear. So, how did this love get reversed? We seem to be doing it to ourselves. Fear of being left behind; fear of not making it into heaven the proper route; fear of sinning; fear of, fear of, fear of; the list is endless.

This fear seems to be keeping us from tapping into the natural vibration we were meant to live by. Even the earth has a natural frequency. And if 'man's' vibration and earth's vibration are to co-exist, through love, think of the utopia we could all experience.

The million (billion) dollar question is, how did we end up in this condition? I believe the answer is, we were lied to and we believed it. Is this all there is? I mean this by, is this that we see with our eyes or believe with our minds, all that exist?

Centuries ago, man believed the planets and stars rotated around the earth. I know that sounds silly in our time, but what is it we are believing that centuries from now, mankind will look upon and say how stupid we were to think certain ways?

There states that there is a veil placed upon mankind. If that is true, and I've heard say that it is now thinning, what if -- and I say, ---what if -- that is why many experience other dimensions. Are there parallel universes? How can we believe that we are the only existing species in our vast universe? Where did all that belief come from? It's as though certain 'men' wanted control of the masses. And what better fear to place on ignorant people (me included) convincing us of lies. It's correct when it is written that there is nothing new under the sun. Whatever we think, we are. Or should I say whatever we believe, that is what we become.

My father-in-law had a saying. He'd say, 'You've told that lie so many times that now even you believe it." How true.

Experience means, "One who has lived with and through it. Direct participage of events. Something personally encountered, undergone, or lived through." (Webster's New Collegiate Dictionary)

You or I may have the knowledge of, let's say, the birth of a child. Only a mother can relate that experience. Women who have never given birth, or any man for that matter, have no idea what it is like. So how can they give a true understanding of what it actually is experienced?

The same is true with ghosts, poltergeists, apparitions, shadow people, sleep paralysis, shapeshifters, etc. Unless you've had the experience, how can you judge what others tell you?

Around a year before my mom passed on, she began questioning her eyesight and her feelings. Now I'll insert here that I never mentioned to either of my parents about our experiences of the supernatural. That stuff was never spoken of. So, to hear my mom tell of her experiences and ask me if I thought she was going crazy, was highly unusual.

My dad had been gone for about four years when she began feeling a presence and seeing strange phenomenon. She was living in an assisted living facility and had a private room. It began with her feeling as if someone was standing behind her chair, that she always sat in. I visited her about four or five times a week, since I worked a few blocks away from the place. She'd ask me, "Is there someone standing behind me?"

At first, I'd brush it off as nothing. She wasn't happy with me doing that and would get irritated at my attitude. She wanted the truth. So, I let her know that I saw no one there. That's when she'd ask me if she was going crazy. Knowing what I know, I'd reassure her that she wasn't. I believed she felt a presence and I told her so. These episodes happened way too often.

Then, she'd tell me of seeing my daddy (her late husband) standing in the apartment, but not alone. There would be a young boy there with him. Now this one freaked me out. Why? A few months after daddy died, I had a profound dream that included my daddy with a young boy as his companion. The dream needn't be discussed here since it is a private understanding for me, but it seems my mom and I were on the same wavelengths with this one.

I'd never told her of the dream, but insisted that I totally believed she was seeing daddy with a young companion. How else could I not?

Mommy would also hear music at time and ask others to find out where it was coming from and turn it off. This I could relate to. Remember me earlier writing about my situation and our daughter?

These next two episodes I cannot explain.

One: She calls me freaking out. It was raining on her outside wall and she had had one of the helpers in the facility come in and take all her pictures off that wall before they were all ruined. The help told me that she was insisting that it was indeed raining in her apartment wall.

Second: It rained outside as well. Now, everyone there insisted that the sun shone that entire day. My mom described that the maple tree outside her window had been covered in ice.

When I arrived at her place the following day and heard the story for the second and third time (the help told me before I had even reached her room), I went to investigate. I had hung bird feeders and gourds for bird houses in that maple tree for her enjoyment. As I examined the tree, the leaves looked shattered.

Okay, how did that happen? Ice? It's the middle of June. Even hail wouldn't coat a leaf, would it? But, the sun shone all day yesterday. No rain was in sight, let alone an ice storm.

So, returning to her room, I saw where the help has placed all her pictures against the inner wall. They kept telling me that, she kept insisting about the rain on the wall would ruin her pictures. So, they appeased her by taking them down. I thanked them and sat down to business with my mom.

She began describing all the chaos that had transpired yesterday, in detail. One thing about my mom, she was sharp as a tack; all there. Nothing passed by her all the way up to her death. So when she spoke of an incident, she knew what she was saying.

Absolutely nothing got past her, plus, she was highly intuitive. I had no idea what to say to her once she told me, in person, what had happened.

While it was actually going on, I was hearing all the commotion between her and the help, via the telephone. So, how could I explain this? I was puzzled. This incident was nothing I'd ever heard of or experienced. And she truly believed it had transpired. So, I told her okay, let me now put the pictures back on the wall and he agreed to that.

All the pictures, except one, were of grandchildren. They were in perfect shape. The large, matted document stood last to be hung, and was facing the wall. Now, I'm about to tell you what really freaked me out, big time.

My daddy retired from the service. He was in several branches during the world war. While in the navy and on a ship once a sailor crosses the equator, he is presented by the commander of the ship a document describing the date and time of the crossing. It is a very unique looking paper. On it is drawings of mermaids, fish, anchors, and such.

And it tells of Davy Jones locker and the mysteries associated with it. We had no idea he even had this, or that it was actually something sailors were presented with. We discovered it when we moved my mom after daddy passed. She didn't even know of its existence. It was just papers in a box that she never went through. So, it was special to all of us.

When I turned the document around from facing the wall, I had a shock. Along the top portion, the document was water damaged! She was correct! But that was the only picture that was harmed.

Now, how do we explain that? Was the veil so thin at that spot, that it was raining, or icing in the parallel universe and some spilled over into ours? I haven't a clue or any answer.

So you can see through these episodes of my mom, that she was experiencing phenomenon beyond her comprehension. She was 'old school' and never went to movies, read many books, or even spoke of the supernatural. She was just a plain, country, woman, who believed in the here and now. Never experiencing such things had her questioning her sanity. Knowing my mom, I believe what she saw and heard was real.

The Old Yellow House

CHAPTER 13

The area we live in governs much of what a person believes. For instance, if we were born and raised in India, Hindu could be the major influence of life. The history and culture of the Vedas, their canonical collections of hymns, prayers, and liturgical formulas of their sacred writings, would be similar to a Christian reading their Bible. What's amazing is that many of the same teachings are extraordinarily the same.

Their writings speak in part, of discarnate souls that can cause havoc in our worldly realm. Some were souls who died suddenly, not expecting to suddenly be at such a point as death. There's, on the other hand, left this reality frightened and instead of moving on to their heavenly abode, remained here on earth, (invisible, of course, to us), and at times attach themselves to familiar surroundings, or people they knew.

Then there are those who cause mischief. We could speak of these as evil spirits, even demons, if you care to go that far. Even Jesus met a man amongst the tombs, possessed by "Legion", meaning many. (Mark 5) and spoke to them, with them answering Him back. He dis-placed them into a herd of swine who couldn't handle such a thing.

So they ran into the sea and drowned themselves in order to be rid of the spirits. Now, since they are already 'dead', I just wonder where these evil spirits went next. It seems that spirits are regional, so I'd hate to be near that area being at the wrong place at the wrong time.

The Hindus even believe in ghost, just as we and other nations believe. Here in the United States, there are hotels, mansions, roadways, and even the Queen Mary docked off the coast of California, advertising ghostly experiences.

Each major city has its share of ghost hunters. I have a friend who kept seeing an apparition outside her home. She called the ghost hunters to come and check out what was actually happening. In their research, they discovered that an elderly man had been hit crossing the street, by a car years ago at the spot he kept appearing at. He, of course, was killed there. So, that would account for a sudden, unexpected, death in which, I guess, no one ever told him that he was dead. He keeps appearing, to this very day. Can he hear us? Your guess is as good as mine. Can he see us? Maybe; maybe not. Maybe he can see glimpse of us, just as we see glimpses of him at times. Those kind of experiences always shake me. I wonder if it shakes them as well?

****

I've read where some believe that we are in a prison, per se. Here we are in a three dimensional world. Are we boxed in along with our minds being in that state also? If we were to broaden our thinking, as many before us did and some are doing now, what would we learn? What could we perceive?

I remember being "preached at", that we are not to know anything other than what we know now. That we are going to only be held accountable for what it is right now, that we know and perceive. Learning about other ways and ideas was of the devil, and we are not to venture into any other teaching. Really? What are they scared of? Us, really knowing truths that can enlighten us? We, breaking the bonds that hold us tightly to "their" way of thinking? If the information is out there for all to know, won't we be held accountable for being so fearful as to not taking that leap of faith? Fear, as I wrote earlier, paralyzes us in such a way, that we just quit. We conjure up our own fear; the news media has us fearful; people can place fear on us; and the list goes on and on. It seems that we are the ones allowing this to grip us. And only me, myself , and I, can break what has been designed to entrap us. Only you can come to the same conclusion. Discern what is happening to us. Then decide what would be right for you. See how it all adds up.

If you are reading this, then discern what I've gone through. I still have a lifetime of questions to ask and search for answers to these questions.

Do we live in a multidimensional universe?

Did I open up a portal by playing on the Ouija Board?

Were those spirits already at the old yellow house, and we just asked them to make themselves known?

If the answer is yes, then how is it the house across the street now is having apparitions and poltergeists? They don't have a board.

And, what if, the new owners of that property we once owned, where the old yellow house use to stand, decided to build a new house on that sight? Would the spirits return and cause them havoc? And/or are they still there wondering around?

I've thrice seen a man standing near the door leading into my kitchen, while I was in my kitchen. He was looking at me when I noticed him. Then, just as soon as I noticed him, he was gone. Of course, upon seeing him, I jumped out of my skin (not literally of course). That is the only incident I've had in the last 20 years. We built this house ourselves on a piece of land that once was a pasture. So, no other structure ever existed here.

The only other incident I can think of could have an explanation of forgetfulness. But, I can argue that point. It being where I know I placed an object in a particular place and when I went back to get it, I never found it. Is there an area where the veil is so thin, that the two dimensions cross and now they have my item on their side? There is another unanswered question.

Is this all there is? Is what we see, what we get? I, for one, say no. There is a whole other realm, or realms, we have never experienced. And I, want to be able to go there when my time is up on this rock.

Again, discern what others think and say. Broaden your horizons. Who knows; truths might start flooding through for you.

"Life isn't happening to you; it's responding to you."

P.S. If you've never seen the movie, "The Others," (2001) starring Nicole Kidman, I'm going to suggest you go rent it and watch it. It truly is an eye opener. Whoever wrote it has had to know something.

About the Author

Joyce Wright lives in Tyro, Mississippi with her husband of 50 years. They have two grown children and 5 grandchildren.